curious about
SERVICE DOGS

BY CARI MEISTER

AMICUS LEARNING

What are you

CHAPTER ONE
1
Helping Paws
PAGE
4

CHAPTER TWO
2
Learning to Help
PAGE
10

curious about?

CHAPTER THREE

Life with Service Dogs
PAGE **16**

Stay Curious! Learn More . . . 22

Glossary 24

Index 24

Curious About is published by
Amicus Learning, an imprint of Amicus
P.O. Box 227, Mankato, MN 56002
www.amicuspublishing.us

Copyright © 2026 Amicus.
International copyright reserved in all countries.
No part of this book may be reproduced in any
form without written permission from the publisher.

Editor: Ana Brauer
Series Designer: Kathleen Petelinsek
Book Designer and Photo Researcher: Sara Hood

Cataloging-in-Publication data is available
from the Library of Congress.
Library Binding ISBN: 9798892008570
Paperback ISBN: 9798892009232
eBook ISBN: 9798892009898
LCCN: 2025012827

Photo Credits: Alamy Stock Photo/Disability Images, 9, William Mullins, 12–13; Dreamstime/Anna Tolipova, 3, 21; Getty Images/fotografixx, 14–15, Huntstock, 18–19, Kelsey Andriot Purcell, 17; Shutterstock/Belish, 2, 11, Csanad Kiss, 7 (second from top), Eric Isselee, 7 (bottom), John Dowling, 10, Natallia Yaumenenka, 7 (second from bottom), New Africa, 5, Roman Chazov, 20, sophiecat, 2, 8, Tanya Consaul Photography, 6, Thomas Ramsauer, 7 (top), yasisam, 7 (middle), 24K-Production, cover, 1; The Noun Project/April Yang, 22, 23, Florent Lenormand, 22, 23

Every effort has been made to contact copyright holders for
material reproduced in this book. Any omissions will be rectified
in subsequent printings if notice is given to the publisher.

CHAPTER ONE 1

What is a service dog?

A service dog is a special helper dog! It helps people who need extra help doing everyday things. They can help people who have trouble seeing, walking, or hearing. They can help people with **PTSD**, too.

Service dogs are trained to help people live more safely and easily.

Can any dog be a service dog?

Service dogs start training young, but many don't finish.

No. A service dog must be calm and good at following directions. Labs and golden retrievers make great service dogs. They love to work and help people! It takes a lot of work to become a service dog. The dogs must be willing to learn new things every day.

LABRADOR RETRIEVER

GOLDEN RETRIEVER

GERMAN SHEPHERD

POODLE

BORDER COLLIE

POPULAR SERVICE DOG BREEDS

7

A service dog can help by pushing the button to cross the street.

HELPING PAWS

What kinds of jobs do service dogs do?

A service dog can open the door when needed.

DID YOU KNOW?
Service dogs can turn on lights, call for help, and even load washing machines!

Service dogs do many jobs! **Guide dogs** help people who are blind walk safely around town. Hearing dogs tell people who are deaf when someone knocks at the door. Some dogs help wheelchair users by picking up dropped items and opening doors.

CHAPTER TWO 2

When do service dogs start training?

LEARNING TO HELP

Service dogs usually start training at around six months old.

When they are puppies! Special families called **puppy raisers** teach them good manners. The puppies learn to be calm in stores, restaurants, and busy places. They must learn not to bark or chase squirrels!

A guide dog in training learns to avoid obstacles.

LEARNING TO HELP

LEARNING TO HELP

What do they learn in school?

Service dogs go to special training schools. They learn important jobs like pushing buttons, picking up things, or helping someone stand. The dogs practice every day for about two years. That's a lot of learning!

DID YOU KNOW?
A service dog must pass a Public Access Test. This tests their ability to be calm in all kinds of settings.

Service dogs in training learn how to help people the right way.

LEARNING TO HELP

DID YOU KNOW?
A service dog can learn more than 50 different **commands**!

This guide dog checks on their person after crossing the road.

LEARNING TO HELP

How do service dogs know what to do?

They learn special commands. They watch their person carefully. They know when help is needed. They even learn when to disobey to keep their person safe! For example, a guide dog won't walk into a busy street, even if told to go.

CHAPTER THREE

LIFE WITH SERVICE DOGS

Where do service dogs go?

They can go everywhere with their person! They can go to schools, stores, restaurants, and even on airplanes. Some dogs wear a special **vest** that says "Service Dog." When you see a service dog, remember not to pet or distract them. They need to stay focused on helping their person.

DID YOU KNOW?
A guide dog can remember hundreds of walking routes.

Service dogs don't have to wear a vest, but many do so people know they are working.

LIFE WITH SERVICE DOGS

How do service dogs act at work?

Service dogs know the difference between work time and playtime.

They are always ready to help! They stay focused on their person. They don't play with other dogs or people. But when they are not working, they get to play and rest.

Service dogs usually work for about eight hours a day.

How long do service dogs work?

For about 10 years. They help their person every day. When they get older and ready to retire, they become pet dogs. Many get to stay with their family and relax! They enjoy getting yummy treats and playtime after many years of working.

A service dog's workday ends when their owner says it's time to stop.

LIFE WITH SERVICE DOGS

STAY CURIOUS!

ASK MORE QUESTIONS

How can I get a service dog?

What is the difference between a service dog and a therapy dog?

Try a BIG QUESTION: How have service dogs changed people's lives?

SEARCH FOR ANSWERS

Search the library catalog or the Internet.
A librarian, teacher, or parent can help you.

Using Keywords
Find the looking glass.

Keywords are the most important words in your question.

?

If you want to know about:
- different types of service dogs, type: SERVICE DOG TYPES
- how to get a service dog, type: SERVICE DOG REQUIREMENTS

LEARN MORE

FIND GOOD SOURCES

Here are some good, safe sources you can use in your research.
Your librarian can help you find more.

Books

Service Dog
by Keith Davidson, 2022.

Service Dogs
by Marie Brandle, 2022.

Internet Sites

ADA: Service Animals
https://www.ada.gov/service_animals_2010.htm
This government website explains rules about service dogs.

Guide Dogs of America
https://www.guidedogsofamerica.org/
This site shows how guide dogs are trained and help people.

Every effort has been made to ensure that these websites are appropriate for children. However, because of the nature of the Internet, it is impossible to guarantee that these sites will remain active indefinitely or that their contents will not be altered.

SHARE AND TAKE ACTION

Create a poster about how to behave around service dogs (like not petting them while they work). Show it to your friends and family.

Interview someone who works with service dogs. Share what you learn with your class.

Make a model of places where service dogs help people, like stores or schools.

GLOSSARY

command A special word that tells a dog what to do.

guide dog A service dog that helps blind people move around safely.

PTSD (post-traumatic stress disorder) A condition that can happen after someone goes through something very scary or upsetting.

puppy raiser A person who teaches a young service dog basic skills.

vest A special jacket that shows a dog is working.

INDEX

breeds, 7
commands, 14, 15
guide dogs, 9, 11, 14, 15, 16
hearing dogs, 9
puppy raisers, 10
training, 5, 6, 10–11, 12, 13
vests, 16, 17
wheelchairs, 9
workdays, 20–21

About the Author

Cari Meister has written many books for children about dogs. She recently rescued a Great Dane puppy from an animal shelter. Cari loves learning about how dogs help keep communities safe. She lives in Vail, Colorado, and sees avalanche dogs at work all winter long.